A

MEXICO
feast and ferment

HAMISH HAMILTON

MEXICO
feast and ferment

TOM OWEN EDMUNDS

WITH AN INTRODUCTION
BY
CARLOS FUENTES

HAMISH HAMILTON · LONDON

... life which offers chances
Ignores the sitters-out and picks the dancers.
- Peter Porter

For my father
David Michael Owen Edmunds, 1924-90
One of life's dancers

HAMISH HAMILTON LTD
Published by the Penguin Group
Penguin Books Ltd, 27 Wrights Lane, London W8 5TZ, England
Penguin Books USA Inc., 375 Hudson Street, New York, New York 10014, USA
Penguin Books Australia Ltd, Ringwood, Victoria, Australia
Penguin Books Canada Ltd, 10 Alcorn Avenue, Toronto, Ontario, Canada M4V 3B2
Penguin Books (NZ) Ltd, 182–190 Wairau Road, Auckland 10, New Zealand

Penguin Books Ltd, Registered Offices: Harmondsworth, Middlesex, England

First published 1992
1 3 5 7 9 10 8 6 4 2

Copyright © Tom Owen Edmunds, 1992
Introduction copyright © Carlos Fuentes, 1992

The moral right of the authors has been asserted

Originated by Bright Arts, Hong Kong
Printed in Hong Kong by Imago Publishing Ltd.

A CIP catalogue record for this book is available from the British Library

ISBN 0–241–13067–0

CONTENTS

ACKNOWLEDGEMENTS

My first acknowledgement must undoubtedly be to Carlos Fuentes, who has immeasurably enhanced this book with his introduction. I am delighted and flattered – thank you.

Many thanks to the Mexican Ambassador H. E. Bernardo Sepulveda, and to Lic. Alicia Cazorla and Lupita Ayala of the Mexican Ministry of Tourism, who were all extremely helpful before I left.

In Mexico I am indebted to Sr. Javier Rivas Garcia of the Ministry of Tourism and to Sra. Gabriela Chavez Morales, who was a magnificent help. Many thanks also to Lic. Victor Flores Olea for all his help and to Miguel Quijano. I am also most grateful to Sr. Juan Valtierra, Sr. Miguel Angel Muñoz, Lic. Pedro Molina Sanchez and to Lic. Valdez in Chihuahua.

However, my biggest thank-you in Mexico must unquestionably go to Gonzalo and Lolita Robles: I can't possibly list all their incredible kindnesses and extraordinary hospitality, so I hope they will settle for a huge *abrazo*. Thank you also to Francisco and to Sr. and Sra. Robles.

Very special thanks must also go to Deo Yarza for having me to stay for five weeks, to Dr Ramon Xirau for introducing me to Carlos Fuentes, to Juan Andrade Nieves (and Fransisco and Victor) for rescuing us in Nayarit, and to our big *amigos* Cuauhtemoc and Chayo Perez Sanchez for their hospitality *y muchas gracias tambien a todas las personas que me ayudaron con* Small-Town Mexico.

I am also indebted to three fellow photographers who helped me with local information (how nice it is in Mexico that there is a fellowship amongst photographers): Pablo Ortiz Monasterio, Patricio Robles Gil and Elizabeth Reid.

Many thanks for advice or assistance in Mexico to Francisco Arce, Mañuel Surebielle, Diego Garcia Elio, Antonio and Pedro Nabarro, Maria Teresa Ugalde and Russell, Cristina Guerrero, Herman Hatch, David Spilsbury, Dr Louis Casagrande, Jacques Tisne, Padre Miguel in Chenalho *y gracias a todos los encargados en Tenejapa*.

In Corpus Christi, USA, I am most grateful to Jim Willis and Laurie and Tony, and to Michael Ashmore and Mac and Kim.

Undoubtedly my greatest thanks in Britain must go to Hamish Hamilton, who have been magnificent, especially Andrew Franklin, who has supported me throughout and who created the decisive impetus initially. Many thanks also to Sophie Ovenden, Sally Abbey and Shona Burns, and to everyone at HH who has worked on *Mexico* or who will do so after this is written; and lastly to Fiona Carpenter, who has been quite wonderful despite my best efforts to drive her to distraction.

Next I must thank Olympus, whose cameras I have always used and which have never let me down whatever I have thrown at them. Many thanks to Barry Taylor, Mark Thackara, Cathryn Fowler, Robin Hinton, Sheila Campion and most especially to Ian Dickens, who has always been tremendously supportive. I am also most grateful to Paul Gates at Kodak for helping to supply me with Kodachrome, my basic film stock.

I must also thank Chris Parrott and Brian Williams at Journey Latin America for considerable assistance with Mexico, as with all my Central and South American travels; Mark Cass and Neil Andrews at the Image Bank, and Chris Kewbank and Catherine Turner at The Special Photographers Gallery (21 Kensington Park Road, London W11 2EU), where limited edition prints of my photographs are available.

I am also very grateful to Jenny Hickman, Beatrice Hollond, William Sieghart and Nicola Roberts for bringing film safely back from location; to John Hickman and Alastair Fothergill for bringing more out; to Conrad Bird for help with the sub-title; to Peter Porter and OUP for permission to use the poem extract in the dedication; and for general advice and assistance to Ian Payne at Lloyds Bank, Jenny Frecknall, Bill Hamilton, Sir John and Lady Morgan, Mary Gibson, Ed Iwanicki, Belinda Hughes-Onslow, Jeremy Drax, Nigel and Shane Winser, Peter Dale, Hugo Williams, Elizabeth Carmichael, Michael Thain, James Blount, Major Patrick Uniacke and Richard Baylis.

My last and greatest thank-you must, as always, be to my wife, Katie Hickman, with whom I travelled and worked for a year in Mexico (her book about our experiences will be published by HarperCollins in mid–1993), *quien, despues de diez años, continuo amar mas con cada secundo que pasa.*

Finally, I would like to point out that all photographs in sensitive areas were taken after having first asked for permission, as I think it is absolutely wrong to ride roughshod over genuinely and passionately held local objections to photography when they exist.

Tom Owen Edmunds
Talycoed, 1992

INTRODUCTION

Tom Owen Edmunds's portfolio of Mexico is as fascinating for what it shows as for what it hides. He has attempted to introduce order in the vast baroque complexity of Mexico. He has layered the country rationally, from north to centre to south. Yet the very fact that several categories – death, bullfights, horseback riders, crucifixions – escape this tidiness and assert their own ritualistic disorder should give us pause.

Modern Mexicans refuse the irrationality, the magic, the sense of the unknown in their own country. They tend to see Mexico as following Western models of development guided by a clearly defined socio-economic plan. The genius of the country is that it constantly thwarts this modernizing or rational goodwill and reasserts, in myriad, ungraspable ways, its right to mystery, to perpetual astonishment and self-discovery.

The beauty of Owen Edmunds's art is that it offers us the dual possibilities of the Mexican psyche in pictorial form. The respectable attempt at introducing order is constantly perverted by the outbreak of chaos, the chasm, the dream, the night, the ritual of a people engaged not so much in telling us what everyone knows, but in discovering what no one knows.

C. A. Burland in his beautiful essays *The Gods of Mexico* was the first to perceive the mandala form (a circular symbol representing the universe) in the art of the ancient Mexicans. As in ancient Indian art, the Mexican designs were based on a pattern of four squares around a centre which is a void. Through these designs, which were often highly intricate, we can understand numerous complex and infinite approaches to time and nature. In ancient Mexico, the mandala of waters indicated the diverse sources of flowing life. A special god, Tlaloc, was the Lord of Waters and his kingdom, Tlalocan, was suspended in the clouds just above the earth. But unlike Western gods who tended to be depicted as a unified whole, Tlaloc's four sources of power were both contradictory and complementary. From the east came the golden rain of the morning; at noon the waters became blue as they moved southwards; at dusk, the world was flooded with red rains from the west; and finally, at night, the crops were blighted by the black rain from the north.

This description, nevertheless, simplifies too much, if we consider that each direction in space had for the ancient Mexicans its own four cardinal points, so that the south had its own north, east, south and west, the north its own south, east, west and north, and so on. If we multiply the directions from each new direction, we are truly immersed in the most concrete

sense of the infinite and are forced, with a shudder, back towards the more simple orientations of the mandala. There is a centre holding all of this together. And the centre is, and must remain, a mystery.

If we now pour, as it were, the images caught by Owen Edmunds into the immense Mexican mandala, we shall see that they are but an invitation to play with them, to reorder them in a creative way, according to both the rigour and the game of the mandala.

You can see these images in the order of their colours, and the colours in the order of daybreak, noon, sunset and night. Attempt it: the morning mist can open this sequence in a blue haze or close it in the deepening dusk of the fog in the mountains of Chiapas. The brightness of noon is in the flight of the butterflies in the valleys of Michoacán or in the birds captured in the head-dress of a boy-flyer from Papantla. The sun returns the oldest stones of Yucatán to golden life, but the glory of noon is forever captured in the bright colours of a blue-pink village wall. A yellow wall, instead, evokes the Indian colour of Death, profusely present in the orange-yellow flowers of the Day of the Dead, the *zampazúchil*, and even if night is defeated by the glow of the electric lights and the cheer of the busy port in Veracruz's main plaza, shadows can create their own time – and self-destructing humanity can erase all notion of day or night, blighting the moon and polluting the sunset, in the detritus-filled smog of Mexico City.

This leads us to yet another invitation I feel in this collection of photographs: the invitation to recreate time, beyond the order of north, centre, south. For the ancient Mexicans, as is now well-known, the mandala of time spread in four directions which evoked four suns or moments of creation: sun of water, sun of wind, sun of fire, sun of earthquake. Four successive catastrophes led us to our present world; under the power of the fifth sun will it too disappear in a cloud of night, a bang of fire, a whimper of *nada*?

The deep sense of sacrifice which both characterized and alienated the universe of the Aztec found its own centre in the troubling questions: will there be a sun tomorrow? Will we ever see the next daybreak? But these questions were premised on a certainty that the world had been created not one but many times. The threat was therefore also a promise. And while the will of the gods was powerful, and the circle of time implacable, the desire of men and women, their work, their dreams, their dignity, was what truly kept the universe alive.

There are two faces of Mexico that have to do with this and these photographs have caught this duality quite brilliantly. The faces of both fatality and defiance look at one another, like the double mask of Janus, in the wonderful series of Day of the Dead photographs, as contrasted with the bullfight images. In the Long Journey of the Dead, through a day and night of homage, respect, sadness and black humour, the people of Mexico do not only commemorate our shared mortality; they forcefully state that death is the origin of life; that without the sacred event of dying, there is no continuity of living; that precisely because death is inevitable, life can be continuous. This celebration of death as part of life is contrasted with the risk of living, the ritual of defying death so as to be worthy of life. The *corrida de toros*, the bullfight, permits men to act before death, to challenge death, instead of merely accepting it passively.

Indian Mexico and Mediterranean Spain are constantly meeting in Owen Edmunds's photographs (I'd love to have a Spanish portfolio by him) and nowhere does this fusion happen on more intimate terms than in the Fiesta of Death and the Fiesta of Bravery: skull and sword, flower and blood, yellow and red, come together, aesthetically, emotionally, to form a cultural whole. But other cultures are waiting in the wings: The Day of the Dead is already invaded by Hallowe'en; a commercial giggle turns the macabre humour sour. But as Mexico increasingly penetrates the United States, will the Aztec and Spanish figures of death finally encompass the singularly unsymbolic facts of North American violence? Whatever the outcome, cultures are made by such encounters and not in isolation, as is proven constantly by the culture of Mexico, which is neither purely Indian nor purely Spanish.

The mandala of time as it spreads in four directions finally returns to a centre called simultaneity. Mexico is a country of simultaneous times, where all past is present, and all history happens, or can happen, today. Rocks are inscribed in the colours of the Stone Age and the Coras perform ancient rituals which have been happening since the origins of their world. A pyramid coexists with a Hard Rock Café, Quetzalcoatl becomes Pepsicoatl, the God of Fire becomes a boy spitting out flames for a few *centavos* in a street corner. But loving couples kiss against the walls of ancient convents, old warriors from the Revolution survive among their souvenirs and, finally, Owen Edmunds seems to be telling us, all the ages of man can be stored in the gaze of an old villager, all the writing of history can be found in the scars of a village wall, and the creation of the world takes place every minute in the forests, the lights or the stones of Mexico.

The centre of the mandala is rich with possibilities. It can become in the blinking of an eye a void, a chasm, or perhaps,

even better, a limit, a frontier, the warning of imminent happenings. All rituals, after all, have to be limited by borders: cricket, baseball, rugby and, certainly, the circle of the bullfighting arena. Terror arrives when the limit is lost, when the diver in Acapulco flies off into the sky only to meet, as it may be, the sea or the jagged rocks beneath the sun. The vultures are perched on a cactus. The workers at the Mexico–US border are perched on a fence. Will they fall into the chasm of nothingness? Will they reach the limit and there create anew, rediscover the sense of all this throbbing life and colour and daring and fatality and sense of presence and living pasts and constant creation?

The artist that is Tom Owen Edmunds sees Mexico. But he sees us all. His eye is posed, for the magnificent instant of a camera's click, on the universal urge to see, understand and yet respect what cannot be seen or understood. These are portraits of the visible world, but even more importantly, perhaps, of the invisible world. *Mexico* is the name of the eye that sees them both.

Carlos Fuentes 1992

San Diego
Mexicali
Tijuana
Ensenada
Nogales
El Paso
Ciudad Juárez
UNITE

BAJA CALIFORNIA NORTE

SONORA

CHIHUAHUA

Hermosillo

Chihuahua

COAH

GULFO DE CALIFORNIA

COPPER
CANYON

Sierra Madre Occidental

Alamos

DURANGO

Los
Mochis

BAJA CALIFORNIA SUR

Culiacán

SINALOA

La Paz

Durango

ZACAT

Mazatlán

PACIFIC

Cabo San Lucas

NAYARIT

Tepic

Puerto
Vallarta
Guadalajara

OCEAN

JALISCO
Colima

COLIMA Si

Cuetzalán

MEXICO

TLAXCALA
Tlaxcala

Mexico City

DISTRITO
FEDERAL
Iztaccíhuatl

Toluca

Popocatepétl
Puebla

Cuernavaca

MORELOS

PUEBLA

Morelos

Taxco

0   240 MIS
0   360 KM

THE NORTH

The cactus, popular symbol of Mexico, grows in spectacular profusion in Baja California,
though a pair of dark turkey vultures makes it a rather more poignant metaphor.

Overleaf: Bizarre plants, specially adapted to the aridity of the Central Desert of Baja
California, in bloom.

Symbolic cave paintings of long-vanished Indians and Jesuit
churches near abandoned mining towns, like Satevo near the Copper
Canyon, attest to the transitory nature of the north which has always
been a frontierland.

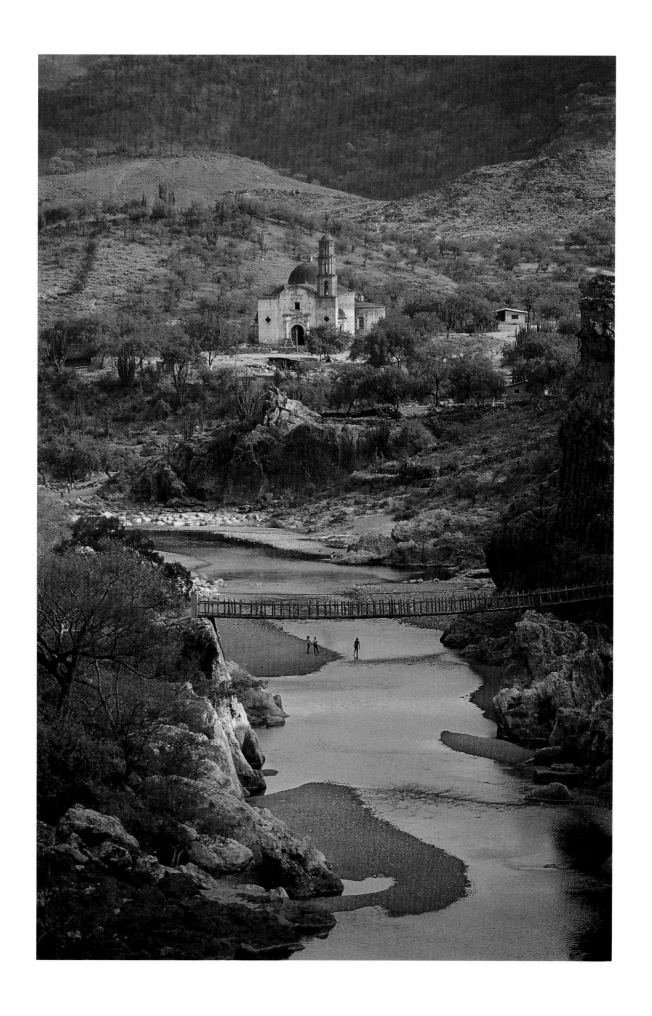

Previous page: Dusk on the border with the US, in Tijuana. Hopeful migrants wait for a US border patrol helicopter to pass before making their illegal dash across no man's land.

The Last Chance Cafés: approaching the Mexican frontier in the US border town of Loredo, the name of the last café is fraught with symbolism for both Americans and Mexicans, while in Tijuana illegal crossing is so commonplace that at a particularly convenient spot a shop is set up selling not only coffee and snacks, but also clothes and even plastic bags to keep people's feet dry when crossing the river.

The outskirts boast new foreign factories but Tijuana itself has retained little of its former glamour and has become a tawdry melting-pot of Mexico's desperate and dispossessed.

After the super-modern shopping mall, this is probably the first sight that greets the millions of tourists who cross the border every year, but neither image is particularly representative of Mexico. In the Avenida Revolución, bars and hawkers compete for the mainly under-age business from San Diego.

Away from the border, the magnet of the US can still be seen in the industrialization, and pollution, of the northern cities, especially Monterrey where the famous architect Luis Barragan built his bright-red Lighthouse of Commerce. *(Above)* In Durango, even Pancho Villa, 'bandit patriot', revolutionary leader and hero of the north, is wreathed in fumes.

Returning home through the arid countryside.

The inaugural trip of a rural bus service in Nayarit.

Even in the north there are several groups of Indians whose hostility and inaccessibility have helped them remain more or less aloof from modern Mexico. In the remote Sierra del Nayar the Cora paint their bodies and don demonic animal masks for their annual fertility rites which coincide with Easter.

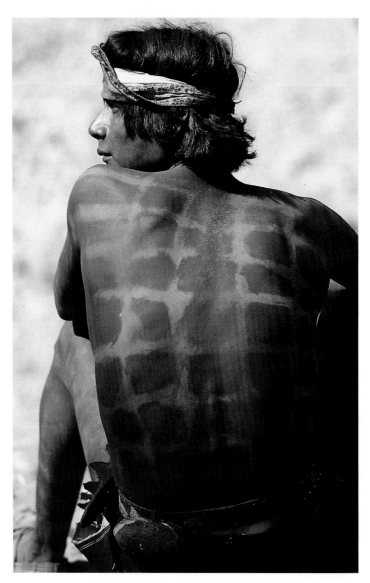

For three days civil law is suspended, authority is turned on its head, and the villages are strictly controlled by *capitanes*, Cora ceremonial officials. A small group, some mocking Mexican fashions with extravagant white sombreros, carry out fertility rituals culminating in a buried man being symbolically brought to life by fellatio from another celebrant dressed as a woman.

DAY OF THE DEAD

For weeks before the Day of the Dead, shops all over Mexico are full of skeletons in every conceivable form, from chocolate coffins and skulls, and personalized sugar skulls, to papier-mâché figures, plates and even skeletal Last Suppers.

The Day of the Dead is a powerful metaphor for Mexico: despite the recent cultural invasion of Hallowe'en from the US and the earlier addition of the Christian feasts of All Saints' Day and All Souls' Day by the Spanish, the pre-Hispanic Celebration of the Dead is still a quintessentially Mexican fiesta.

In Patzcuaro a girl buys Zampazúchil flowers to attract the souls of the dead.

Elaborate offerings are made at the graves of departed relatives, whose souls are believed
to return during the silent night-long wake, guided by incense and the light
of the candles.

Overleaf: Dawn breaks over the Day of the Dead, ending the all-night vigil of the
Purépecha Indians in the cemetery of the island of Janitizio. It is a strangely moving
climax to a fiesta which celebrates not death, but life's triumph over death.

THE CENTRE

The baroque façade of San Francisco Church and the cloisters and carved window of the churrigueresque chapel of Aranzazú in San Luis Potosi.

Huastec Indians, distant cousins of the Mayas, at the Sunday market in Ciudad Santos
near San Luis Potosi.

Walking to the Sunday market at Ciudad Santos.

The Sierra Madre Oriental in northern Puebla, whose inhospitable terrain has helped
preserve the identity of several groups of Indians.

A man waits at a corner and a young Nahua Indian girl carries
a child in Cuetzalán. The Nahuas are the most populous Indian
group; their language was spoken by the Aztecs.

Traditional medicine, both herbal and spiritual, is still very strong in Mexico, especially amongst Indian communities. At the weekly market in Cuetzalán a travelling medicine man does a brisk business in balm of salamander.

Impromptu markets spring up at every local fiesta such as the feast of St Andrew in San Andrés. Amongst the sacred dances performed is the spectacular *voladores* of the Totonac Indians. Its pagan form and symbolism remain intact; the flautist at the top of the pole represents the sun and the four fliers: the earth, air, fire and water. Only now it is performed in the courtyard of the church.

At the end of the fiesta, Quetzales dancers return home. The elaborate head-dresses mimic the plumes of the resplendent Quetzal which adorned the pre-Columbian deity Quetzalcóatl.

Previous page: A lady sells *quesadillas* outside an old colonial house in Puebla.

A private courtyard with hand-painted tiles for which Puebla is famed.

Spanish colonial architecture in the heart of Puebla.

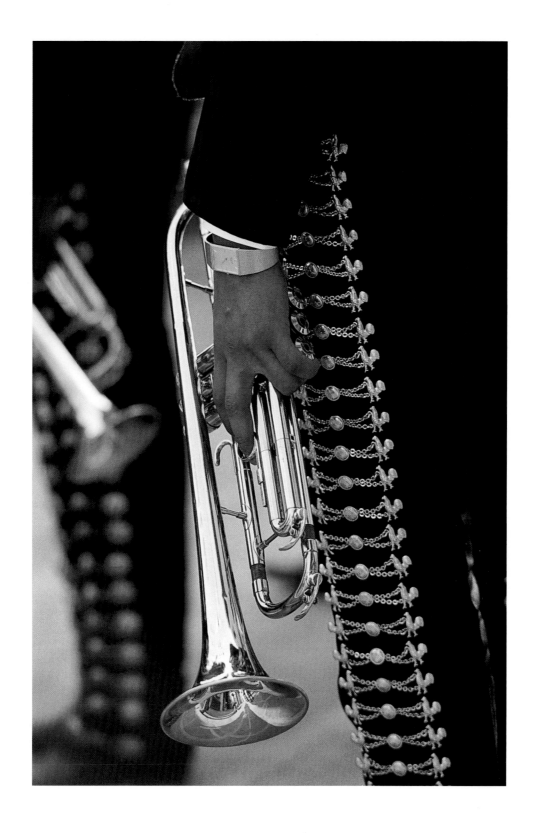

Mariachi is the heartbeat of Mexico. Each year, at the feast of St Cecilia, patron saint of music, Mariachi players gather for a procession around the streets of Puebla, donning in her honour their finest suits.

A monk in the courtyard of the Parroquia de San Andreas, Calpan.

The Moorish arch of the open-air chapel of San Francisco Monastery in Tlaxcala, one of
the oldest Catholic buildings in the New World.

A gilded altarpiece in the church of San Francisco Javier, Tepotzotlán. Popocatépetl, 'Smoking Mountain', rising above the sixteenth-century Parroquia in Calpan.

The famous Pyramid of the Moon standing at the end of the Street of the Dead in
Teotihuacán. This civilization reached such size and sophistication that by AD 600 its
population outnumbered Rome's. Though abandoned in the eighth century, Teotihuacán
was revered by the Aztecs, who called it 'The Place Where Men Become Gods'.

A figure of Quetzalcóatl, the 'Plumed Serpent' and pre-eminent deity of Meso-America,
in the temple of Quetzalcóatl at Teotihuacán.

A stone statue, over four metres high, of a warrior representing Quetzalcóatl as the Morning Star at Tula, capital of the Toltec civilization. The recently discovered 'Mural of Battle' at Cacaxtla and a mural of Tlaloc, the rain-god, at Teotihuacán.

Previous page: Flame-thrower at a traffic light in Toluca; a desperate way to earn a
meagre living.

A shrine to the blind child Saint Santo Niño Cieguecito in the Senora market and the
gruesome Mummy Museum in Guanajuato pander to the dark side of the
Mexican psyche.

Overview of Guanajuato, an exquisite Spanish colonial silver town and scene of one of
Padre Hidalgo's greatest victories in the War of Independence. A *cantina* (a Mexican bar)
in Guanajuato.

Overleaf: Street in Guanajuato near the Callejón del Beso.

On the Día de las Flores in Guanajuato lovers gather from early morning to promenade
and present bouquets to sweethearts in the Jardín de la Uníon. Free drinks are dispensed
from elaborate shrines to the Virgin de los Dolores.

Previous page: Monarch butterflies in a wood in Michoacán.

Magazines with real decapitated heads on the cover are a manifestation of the Mexican obsession with death, visible even in holiday towns such as Acapulco. The machismo of flaunting death proves irresistible for Acapulco's and Mazatlán's famous High Divers.

Whole swathes of the Pacific Coast have become tourist resorts catering chiefly to Americans. In Puerto Vallarta a *chicle*-seller (chewing-gum seller) stops customers outside the Hard Rock Café, while a balloon-seller promenades along the front at dusk.

In Cabo San Lucas a Brown Pelican stretches just opposite
Lovers' Beach.

Away from the resorts, Mexico reasserts itself rapidly.

Wrecked cars are often displayed on the roadside as 'monuments to the imprudence of dangerous driving'.

Rural Mexico: a small rural town in Jalisco, threshing with horses in Michoacán, and a
donkey laden with straw.

Two farmers in Guerrero's remote and inhospitable Tierra Caliente. The 'hot country' is so named not just for the intense heat but also because of its long history of relentless blood-feuds.

A lone guitar player strolls through the Jardín de la Unión in Guanajuato while ten or more bands can be playing at any one moment in the cosmopolitan plaza of the port-town of Veracruz.

The plaza is the soul of any Mexican town and none more so than Veracruz, whose plaza
seldom sleeps.

HOLY WEEK

The procession in neighbouring San Miguel de la Camana.
First light on Palm Sunday in Jamiltépec on the Oaxaca coast sees the start of the week-
long explosion of fiestas celebrating Semana Santa, or Holy Week, throughout Mexico.

After the service in Jamiltépec a Mixtec Indian woman holds her palm cross, while a *palmero* walks through the town distributing crosses to outlying houses.

On Wednesday night in Taxco figures of Christ are brought
out of the churches and quietly processed through the town
accompanied by an executioner.

Thursday night in Ixtapalapa sees the enactment of the Last Supper and the procession to
the Garden of Gethsemane accompanied by young boys with candles, who on Good
Friday morning march with heavy, blackened, wooden crosses and crowns of real thorns.

On Good Friday in Ixtapalapa over 300 people enact in detail the last hours of Christ, watched by tens of thousands of the faithful. To play Christ is both a great honour and an enormous physical challenge, though others can afford to take their roles less seriously.

As the drama of the Passion unfolds and Christ is stripped and beaten, sentenced to
death, and finally crucified, the atmosphere becomes increasingly highly charged.
Suddenly, the prayers, and the tears, are for real.

On Saturday after a brief show of bravado, revenge is taken on Judas. In Cuajimalpa two figures of Judas are hung from the church and whipped, and finally an effigy of Judas is exploded.

Perhaps because Mexicans have traditionally identified more with suffering than salvation, Easter Sunday is a more low-key affair. At the service in Tetela del Volcan young men dress as women and then stage masked dances. In Yecapixtla the Moorish Spanish *Chinelos* dance is performed and Holy Week ends with the saints being taken from the churches in procession through the streets.

MEXICO CITY

In the south of Mexico City stands the beautiful old Spanish
colonial suburb of St Angel, once the residence of Cortez.

A floating Mariachi band and flower-seller in Xochimilco, the Venice of Mexico City. In Nahuatl, Xochimilco means 'the place where flowers grow'.

In the trendy Zona Rosa beautiful restaurants and chic women vie for attention. Even in the centre of Mexico City it is possible to enjoy a moment of tranquillity in the Alameda Park.

The harsh reality of life for a young boy in the world's largest city. Little of the money
guarded by this machine-gun-toting policewoman near the Zócalo will filter its way
down to Mexico City's huge under-class.

Begging can be the only way to survive in a city where all the police, judiciary and politicians are assumed to be corrupt. For Mexican women there is an ever-present hassle of another kind.

Mexico City is famous for its smog and for its traffic, neither of which disappoint. At peak times a multitude of hawkers walk down the lines of stationary cars under the Angel of Independence in Reforma.

Traffic, poverty and Mexican exuberance have spawned a rich sub-culture in the congested streets of the capital.

Poor *barrios* surround Mexico City for miles on every side, growing daily. They may look grim from the outside but parts of older *barrios*, such as Santa Fé, have made great efforts to improve.

Houses are built one on top of another on the crowded slopes of barrio Santa Fé, where construction never ceases. Along the main road a man picks through the rubbish while another walks past a modern muralist's expression of the resentment that ferments below the surface.

Demonstrations, political and economic, are becoming commonplace as Mexicans become more politically involved. On Labour Day, riot police temporarily halt opposition protestors marching towards the official government rally in the Zócalo.

After a brief skirmish, the protesters reaching the Zócalo after the parade has ended tear down huge pro-government banners and burn them. Like other demonstrations, it is angry but essentially good-natured.

For a people of genuinely mixed race, Independence Day is a powerful unifying symbol
and provides Mexicans a chance to vent their considerable nationalistic fervour.

The Eagle and Serpent of Mexico's national crest shine bright over the main road to the
Zócalo and the Cathedral for Independence Day.

Huge crowds gather in the Zócalo at midnight on 15 September to hear the President
deliver 'El Grito', Hidalgo's famous Independence Cry. The concluding roar of 'Viva
Mexico' is a mystical moment for Mexicans.

On 20 November the President and other dignitaries once again line the balcony of the
Presidential Palace, this time to mark Revolution Day. Parades may help provide
temporary escape from the burdens of life but never from ever-present authority.

Mexico's greatest passion is reserved for the Virgin of Guadalupe, Patroness of Mexico, who appeared to an Indian convert called Juán Diego in 1531. Pilgrims converge from all over Mexico, some walking for many weeks, to celebrate her festival on 12 December.

The day dawns over hundreds of pilgrims with blankets and banners sleeping rough in the courtyard of the Basilica. This is the most visited Christian shrine in the world after the Vatican.

Penitents walk the last five kilometres, or sometimes more, on their knees along the
Calzada de Guadalupe. If they collapse, Red Cross officials patch them up and they
continue on their way. The object of their devotion is the cloak of Juán Diego on which
the image of the Virgin miraculously appeared from rose petals gathered at
her instruction.

Outside the Basilica the courtyard overflows with tributes to the Virgin, some as
souvenirs, but mostly in the form of dance. Nothing symbolizes the cultural and
theological melting-pot of Mexico better than the increasingly popular *Concheros* Dance.
Invented by the Jesuits from remnants of pre-Hispanic dances, it is performed by modern
Mexicans dressed as pagan cannibalistic Aztecs. One holds a banner of the Virgin but
there is no role for the Spanish who brought her from Guadalupe and gave Mexico
half its blood.

TORO AND CHARRO

Mexican rodeos, or *charreadas*, are held throughout the country.
Most popular in Jalisco, they are a celebration of skills still
needed in the countryside. A rider straps on leather leggings in
preparation for the first event, the *Cala de Caballo*, stopping
dead from a gallop.

The ladies have their own events called *escaramuza charra*, a form of team dressage. A *charro* deomonstrates his prowess with a lasso and a young boy instructs his brother.

Overleaf: The *coleadero,* or 'thriller', is a *charro* speciality. It involves grabbing the tail of a galloping bull and tossing it on to its back.

The *charreada* may be more uniquely Mexican but the Fiesta Brava – bullfighting – is even more popular. Mexico City boasts the largest Plaza de Toros in the world and there is something in this exotic dance with death which strikes a chord in Mexicans. First the *torero* sizes up the bull with a large cape and next the mounted *picador* encourages it to charge so that he can weaken it with his lance.

After a show of bravado to attract the bull the *torero*, or one of his assistants, rushes at the
bull and plants three pairs of *banderillas* in the top of its back as it charges.

Finally the *torero* dedicates the bull and is given sixteen
minutes to impress the crowd with daring passes before
despatching it. Errors are greeted with howls of derision and, if
bored, the crowd may lavish their admiration instead on a
beautiful spectator with raucous shouts of *'torera torera'* .

Aficionados do not come to see a bull being killed; they seek artistry in the mastery of the *torero* and the courage of the bull. But when the *torero* raises his sword (above) and the time for the kill comes, it is not always the bull's blood that gets spilled first.

SMALL-TOWN MEXICO

This is a portrait of an unexceptional small Mexican town, perhaps just a large village,
in the countryside of Jalisco.

It is ranching country and the main street rings to the cracking of hooves as often as it
does to the clatter of engines.

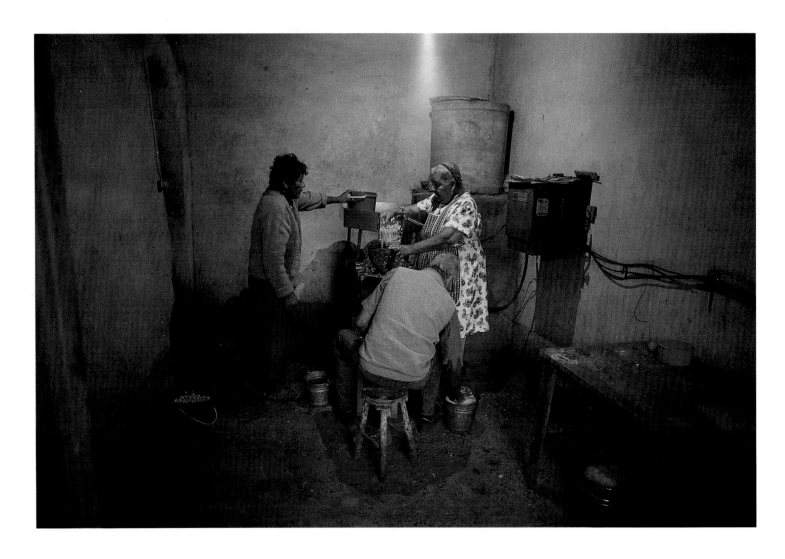

The first to start work is the maize grinder in the tortilla shop, followed at dawn by one of the general stores.

A little later the tortillas, staple of the Mexican diet, are on sale and the general store in
the plaza has opened.

Vicente Ruelas Cortez heads off on his donkey while Antonio de Los Santos prepares a
slaughtered pig and boils up the offal to make *botanas*.

Cuauhtémoc Perez Sanchez owns the butcher's shop, a ranch and a hardware store, but
first and foremost he is a *charro*. His house on the plaza is the oldest in town, complete
with the original gun slits which protected it from bandits.

The village tramp warms himself by Antonio's fire outside the butcher's shop.

At midday the sober exterior of the old building in the plaza opposite the butcher's resounds to the screams of school-children visiting the games room inside on their way home.

The twin idols of modern Mexico hang in the plaza while the *cantina* is entertained by a
group from the next-door town.

Almost opposite the *cantina*, Aurora Cardenas poses with her collection of religious
artifacts, including a 300-year-old figure of the Virgin. Nearby, Felix Arana Toscano
looks out at the siesta-bare street. After the revolution he fought in the War of the
Cristeros, helping to protect priests and the church against the anti-clerical government
of the 1920s. His portrait from that time hangs on the wall behind.

The mayor inside his office is attended by the town's four policemen sitting outside. This
area has had a very lawless past: Porfidio Torres Nuño, woman-robber and ex-
government-employed bandit-hunter, killed his first man when he was thirteen.

Twelve-year-old Jorje drives with impunity. Ramon, the village urchin, skips school and
Temo uses the last light of day to practise with his lasso.

THE SOUTH

Monte Albán, hill-top capital of the Zapotec civilization, outside Oaxaca.
The gilded stucco roof of the church of Santo Domingo in Oaxaca, which depicts the
family tree of Santo Domingo de Guzmán, founder of the Dominicans.

Previous page: A church rests at the foot of the dry brown hills surrounding the Oaxaca Valley.

Much is still mysterious in Mexico; the tranquil waters of Catemaco's lake belie its status as the witchcraft capital of Mexico. The mysterious negroid nose and jaguar mouth of the massive basalt heads buried at La Venta by the Olmecs, the first great civilization of Meso-America.

Witchcraft, both black and white, is still very prevalent in Mexico. In Catemaco a witch prepares his black-magic room, complete with dolls and hair clippings, for a satanic ritual. Elsewhere in the south people perform *limpias* (ritual cleansings) in caves and still worship stalactites, though they have now been given saints' names.

The tropical isthmus of Tehuantepec is the home of the imposing Tehuana Indians. They are renowned not only for eating armadillos and iguanas but also for being a matriarchal society, a rarity indeed in macho-dominated Mexico.

Mérida, capital of the Yucatán, preserves much of its colonial inheritance, including old street signs; but it is the gentle nature of the Mayas which sets it apart from most Mexican cities.

The Convent of St Anthony de Padua in Izamal, established in 1533, is one of the oldest convents in the New World. The Spanish demolished the Mayan pyramid which stood there before and used the same stones to build the convent on top.

In the nineteenth century Yucatán plantation-owners grew fabulously wealthy by
exporting henequen for rope. Their opulent *haciendas* still survive but some are only fit
for impromptu classes.

Fiestas play a pivotal role in Mexican society. For Indians it is a reaffirmation of their culture and community. In the tiny Mayan village of Dzitas a large, white, ceremonial cone is carried between the houses of the fiesta patrons and a local bullfight is staged in a makeshift plaza.

A fisherman chases his pet pelican in the backyard of his house in the little port of Rio Lagartos. The atmosphere here is distinctly tropical.

The white beaches of the Yucatán's Caribbean coast attracted settlers long before today's
tourists. Tulum, 'City of Dawn', was a sacred fortress town for the sea-trading Mayas,
still occupied when the Spanish invaded.

A stucco head on the Palace at Palenque and a corbelled arch leading to the Nun's
Quadrangle at Uxmal attest to the considerable artistic accomplishment of the Mayas,
one of the world's great ancient civilizations.

Figures of the Mayan rain-god, Chac, covering the façade of the Codz Pop Temple at
Kabah in the drought-prone Puuc Hills. The Pyramid of the Magician at Uxmal.

The Mayan ruin of Yaxchilán in the Chiapas rainforest. Widespread deforestation has claimed most of Mexico's jungle and reduced the Amazonian-featured Lacandones Indians to just a few hundred, most of whom now belong to Evangelical Christian groups.

A few small isolated pockets of cloud forest still survive in Chiapas, such as on the slopes of Tacaná Volcano near the border with Guatemala.

A traditional Chamulan Indian house. Chiapas, formerly part of Guatemala, is a state
apart in Mexico. Its population is 20 per cent pure-blooded Indian. The Chiapas
Highlands are the stronghold of the fiercely independent, and sometimes hostile, Indians
who speak Maya-related languages and little Spanish.

Even amongst the same ethnic group the dress can differ radically from one village to the next. In Oxchuc traditional clothes survive despite the onslaught of television a few miles away in San Cristóbal de las Casas, the former colonial capital of Chiapas.

Centuries of domination and savage exploitation by the Spanish, by big landowners and now by tourism have left the Indians extremely suspicious of outsiders. In San Cristóbal an Indian woman walks under the imposing façade of Santo Domingo church while another sells cigarettes outside a hotel.

Previous page: A Chamulan Indian in colonial San Cristóbal.
At the Sunday market in the Tzotzil village of San Juán Chamula just before Carnival the
blue of the Chamulan women and the white of their menfolk mix with the bright pink of
their Tzotzil neighbours, the Zinacantecos.

The pre-Lent celebration of Carnival is a big fiesta in the Chiapas Highlands but only because it coincides with the pre-Hispanic observance of the five 'Lost Days' of the Mayan calendar. In the hill-top Tzotzil village of San Andrés celebrants emerge through the mist to witness the beginning of Carnival. The *encargados*, ceremonial officials who have paid for the fiesta, gather in front of the church for the celebration to be blessed. The crosses, however, have circles at the end, making them identical to the pagan Maya Tree of Life.

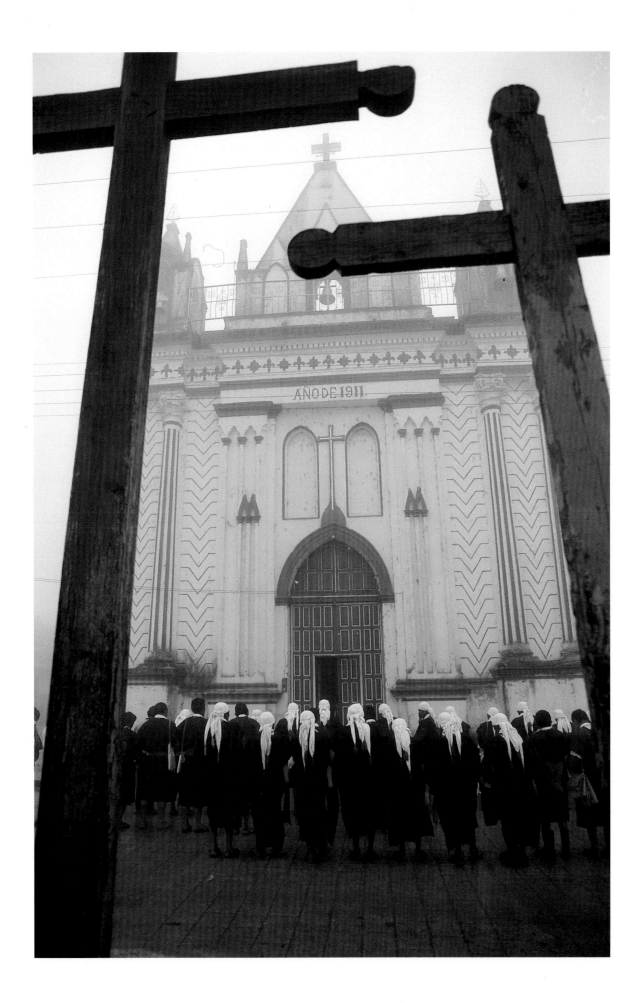

During Carnival in Chenalhó bands of wandering minstrels in monkey-skin hats and Napoleonic frock coats entertain the crowds. Tzotzil horsemen gallop under turkeys suspended above the streets before they are eventually decapitated and their heads paraded around the village.

In the Tzeltal village of Tenejapa, Carnival lasts ten days. The *Encargados*, with staffs of office, and the women gather to await the dancers.

Drink is a vital ingredient of Tzeltal rituals, though it is meant to be as much spiritual as hedonistic.

Previous page: Carnival dancers at Tenejapa.

After the dances some succumb to alcohol.

The younger boys meanwhile chase and lasso the Carnival cow belonging to one of the
two groups of dancers.

After a suspicious start you may find that by the end of the day the hand of friendship is being extended – perhaps not a bad metaphor for Mexico itself.